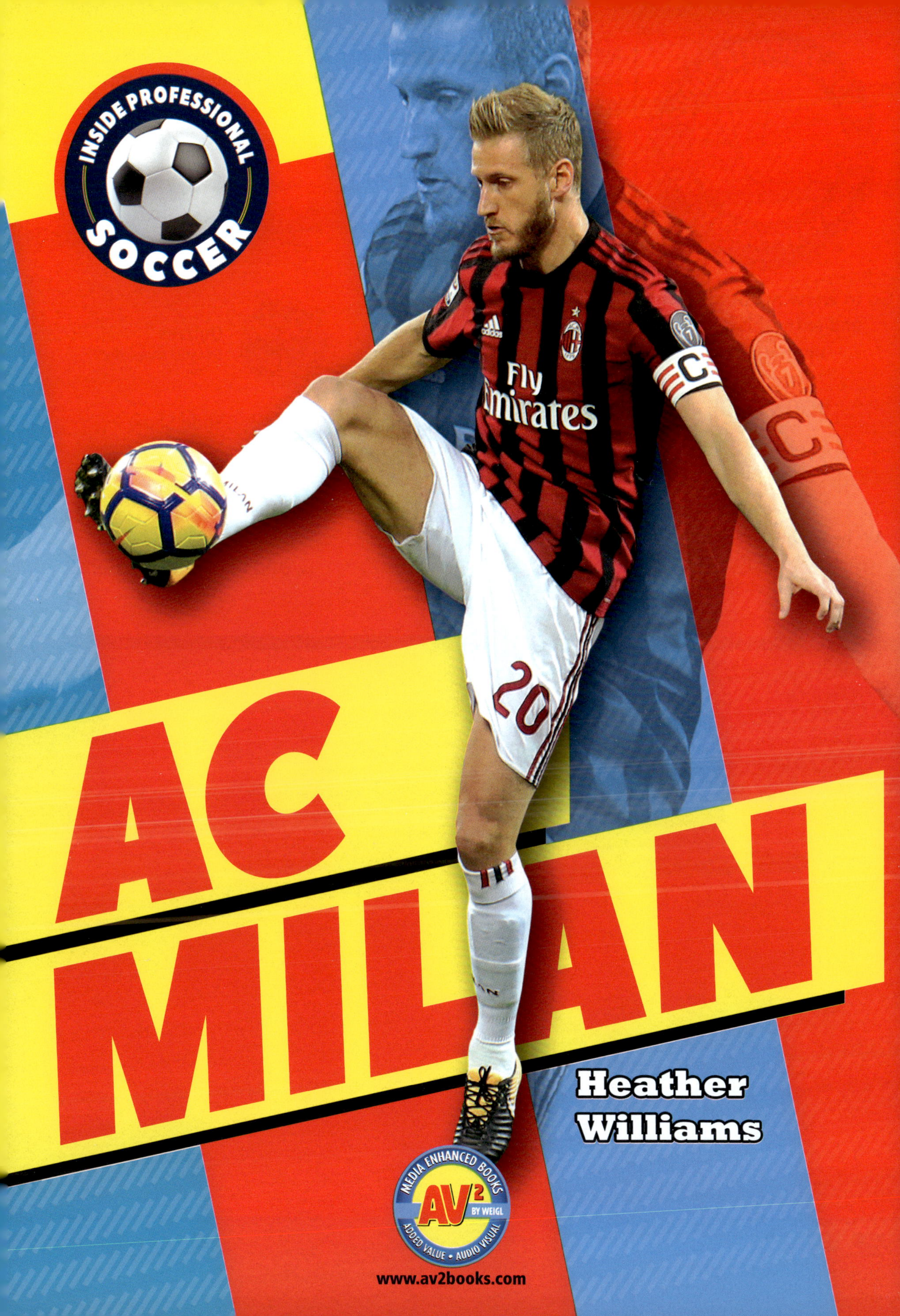
INSIDE PROFESSIONAL SOCCER
AC MILAN
Heather Williams
MEDIA ENHANCED BOOKS
AV2 BY WEIGL
ADDED VALUE • AUDIO VISUAL
www.av2books.com

Go to **www.av2books.com**, and enter this book's unique code.

BOOK CODE

AVH54796

AV² by Weigl brings you media enhanced books that support active learning.

AV² provides enriched content that supplements and complements this book. Weigl's AV² books strive to create inspired learning and engage young minds in a total learning experience.

Your AV² Media Enhanced books come alive with...

Audio
Listen to sections of the book read aloud.

Key Words
Study vocabulary, and complete a matching word activity.

Video
Watch informative video clips.

Quizzes
Test your knowledge.

Embedded Weblinks
Gain additional information for research.

Slide Show
View images and captions, and prepare a presentation.

Try This!
Complete activities and hands-on experiments.

... and much, much more!

Published by AV² by Weigl
350 5th Avenue, 59th Floor
New York, NY 10118
Website: www.av2books.com

Copyright © 2019 AV² by Weigl
All rights reserved. No part of this publication may be reproduced, stored in a retrieval system, or transmitted in any form or by any means, electronic, mechanical, photocopying, recording, or otherwise, without the prior written permission of the publisher.

Library of Congress Control Number: 2018930415

ISBN 978-1-4896-7790-7 (hardcover)
ISBN 978-1-4896-7791-4 (softcover)
ISBN 978-1-4896-7792-1 (multi-user eBook)

Printed in the United States of America in Brainerd, Minnesota
1 2 3 4 5 6 7 8 9 0 22 21 20 19 18

022018
120817

Project Coordinator: John Willis   Designer: Terry Paulhus

Every reasonable effort has been made to trace ownership and to obtain permission to reprint copyright material. The publishers would be pleased to have any errors or omissions brought to their attention so that they may be corrected in subsequent printings.

The publisher acknowledges Getty Images, Alamy, and Wikimedia as its primary image suppliers for this title.

CONTENTS

Introduction

Milan, Italy, is known for its art, architecture, and fashion. Many well-known monuments and buildings are located there. It is also home to a soccer **club** called *Associazione Calcio Milan*, or "AC Milan." Soccer is called **football** in most European countries.

AC Milan is one of the top-performing teams in the **Serie A** division. Serie A is among the four highest-ranking soccer leagues in the world. Milan has won the **Scudetto** 18 times. The team has also won around 50 Italian, European, and Fédération Internationale de Football Association (**FIFA**) World **titles**. Milan attracts some of the world's greatest soccer players.

In a game against Pescara in 2012, Milan midfielder Antonio Nocerino scored a goal just 35 seconds after the starting whistle.

AC Milan has been a source of excitement for soccer fans for more than 100 years. Its dramatic local rivalries keep fans entertained each season. Although the team has not been very successful in recent years, Milan still has millions of fans around the world. Milan is Italian soccer at its best.

Center Leonardo Bonucci is best known for his time with Juventus. He was signed by Milan in 2017.

AC MILAN

Arena Stadio Giuseppe Meazza (San Siro)

Division Serie A

Head Coach Gennaro Gattuso

Location Milan, Italy

FIFA World Club Cups 1

Nicknames *Rossoneri* ("The Red and Black"), *Il Diavolo* ("The Devil")

5 Italian Cups

3 Intercontinental Cups

2 Retired Numbers

3 Consecutive Seasons as Top Scorer by Gunnar Nordahl

80,018 Seats in San Siro Stadium

History

In 1963, Cesare Maldini captained the Rossoneri to victory in the European Cup at London's Wembley Stadium.

AC Milan was formed in 1899. The club was founded by Alfred Edwards and Herbert Kiplin. They were Englishmen who had moved to Italy for business. The two men called the team Milan Foot-Ball and Cricket Club. The club won its first Italian Football trophy in 1901.

Milan won two more national championships in 1906 and 1907. A disagreement caused a split in the club in 1908. Some players formed a new club called Inter Milan. Milan was not very successful after the split with Inter Milan. They did not win another title until 1950. Today, Milan and Inter Milan are fierce rivals. The two clubs compete in a **derby** at San Siro twice a year.

From 1950 until the late 1970s, Milan won 16 Italian and European titles. However, in 1980, some of the club's players were involved in a **scandal**. They were accused of paying referees to help their team win matches. As a consequence, Milan was moved to a lower division called Serie B. Milan returned to Serie A in 1983 and has remained there since. They won the Scudetto in 2007 and again in 2011. AC Milan has not qualified for the championship since 2011.

AC Milan was the only Italian team to qualify for the very first European Cup in 1955.

The Arena

100,000

When San Siro was renovated in 1935, designers planned for the stadium to hold 150,000 people. They later settled on just under 100,000.

It cost around 5 million Italian lire, less than $3,000, to build San Siro in 1926.

San Siro's nickname is "The Temple of Soccer." It is the largest stadium in Italy. San Siro is the home stadium to both AC Milan and Inter Milan. The Italian National team sometimes plays there as well. Many championship games are played at San Siro. It also hosted games in the 1934 and 1990 FIFA World Cup competitions.

San Siro was built in 1926. It was renamed Stadio Giuseppe Meazza in 1980, after a well-known player from Milan, Giuseppe Meazza. However, teams and fans still refer to it as San Siro. The stadium was renovated in 1935 and 1954. In 1990, it was renovated yet again, for the FIFA World Cup.

San Siro is one of Italy's most unique soccer stadiums. Eleven concrete towers support the seats and the roof. The roof design includes four bright red steel beams that stick out from the four corners. San Siro is also the site of an AC Milan museum. The museum contains **memorabilia** from the club's history. Many famous musicians, including Beyoncé and Bruce Springsteen, have performed at San Siro.

Mondo Milan, "The World of Milan," is an interactive museum that uses real objects and cutting-edge technology to immerse visitors in AC Milan history.

Where They Play

Arena
Stadio Giuseppe Meazza (San Siro)

Location
Milan, Italy

Broke Ground
1925

Completed
September 19,1926

Field Design
The **pitch** is surrounded by more than 80,000 numbered seats. All seats are covered while the playing field is open to take advantage of natural lighting.

Features
- Seating areas are identified by color (red, blue, green, and orange)
- 300 Sky Box seats and 304 VIP seats
- Playing surface is GrassMaster hybrid grass, which is made of real grass and artificial fibers

SERIE A DIVISION TEAMS

1 Atalanta *(Bergamo, Italy)*
2 Benevento *(Benevento, Italy)*
3 Bologna *(Bologna, Italy)*
4 Cagliari *(Cagliari, Italy)*
5 Chievo *(Verona, Italy)*
6 Crotone *(Crotone, Italy)*
7 Fiorentina *(Florence, Italy)*
8 Genoa *(Genoa, Italy)*
9 Hellas Verona *(Verona, Italy)*
10 Inter Milan *(Milan, Italy)*
11 Juventus *(Turin, Italy)*
12 Lazio *(Rome, Italy)*
★13 Milan *(Milan, Italy)*
14 Napoli *(Naples, Italy)*
15 Roma *(Rome, Italy)*
16 Sampdoria *(Genoa, Italy)*
17 Sassuolo *(Sassuolo, Italy)*
18 SPAL *(Ferrara, Italy)*
19 Torino *(Turin, Italy)*
20 Udinese *(Udine, Italy)*

The Uniforms

In 2016, AC Milan sold about $650,000 worth of jerseys.

HOME

Milan's colors have been red and black since the team was formed in 1899. The home **kit** includes the team's recognizable red-and-black-striped jersey and white shorts. AC Milan's badge, a patch with the team's logo, is located on the upper left chest of the jersey. Milan's logo was the flag of Milan for many years. Today, it is an oval containing the club's colors and a small red cross. At the top are the letters ACM, the acronym of the club's name. At the bottom is the year the club was founded.

The club's away kit is all white. The white uniforms are considered lucky by players and fans. Milan has won six out of eight Champions League finals while wearing them. An alternate uniform is all black with red trim. It is rarely used in games.

Emirates Air is the official sponsor of AC Milan and hosts training camps and tournaments for the team each season.

Goalie Gear

Goalies often have to dive for saves, so many wear padded shorts to protect them from high-impact falls.

Goalkeepers must stand out from field players and officials. Goalies usually wear long sleeves and brightly colored jerseys. In recent games, the keepers for Milan have guarded the goal in gold, black, and green jerseys. They can either wear pants or shorts. Most wear special goalkeeping gloves. These gloves have rubbery surfaces to help them grip the ball. Some goalkeeper gloves contain plastic spines to protect keepers' hands from injuries.

Gianluigi "Gigio" Donnarumma is the starting goalkeeper for Milan. Born in 1999, he is the second-youngest goalkeeper to play in the Serie A division. Donnarumma is considered one of Italy's most exciting goalkeepers. Even though he is so young, he is very skilled. Soccer experts believe he has a great future in the sport. Donnarumma's older brother, Antonio, is also a goalkeeper for Milan.

Gianluigi Donnarumma's 2017 contract with AC Milan included an agreement that the team would also sign Antonio Donnarumma.

The Coaches

Before Gennaro Gattuso became a coach, he played professional soccer. He played the most games for AC Milan.

Milan has seen nearly 50 different coaches since its formation. Some lasted only a season. A few stayed for several years. A handful of coaches left and returned to their positions multiple times. Many of the coaches were former players for the club.

NEREO ROCCO Nereo Rocco became Milan's coach for the first time in 1961. While he was coach, Milan won its first Intercontinental Cup. Rocco served as a coach for Milan three different times. He coached 459 matches over nine total seasons. He was Milan's most winning coach. Many consider him to be one of the greatest football coaches of all time.

HERBERT KIPLIN Milan's first coach was the team's founder, Herbert Kiplin. In 1891, he became the first Englishman to play football for another country. Before he started AC Milan, Kiplin played on his employer's team, Internazionale Torino. He coached and played for Milan for nine seasons and won three titles.

ARRIGO SACCHI Arrigo Sacchi never played professional soccer. Before Sacchi became a coach, he was a shoe salesman for many years. He was appointed head coach of Milan in 1987. Milan won eight major titles during his time as coach. Some people considered Milan to be the greatest professional team of all time during the four years Sacchi was coach.

Fans Around the World

Ultras typically sit in the *curva*, or seats behind the goals. During the game, they try to cheer better and louder than other team's fans.

Many people around the world support AC Milan. The club has more than 33 million followers on social media. Some Italian football fans get very excited about their teams. These fans are called **ultras**. Ultras hold up large, colorful flags and banners during matches. They also sing songs and make words or shapes in the stands using colored signs. Ultras have their own seating areas at games. They march into the stadium singing and chanting.

One of Italy's oldest groups of ultras was *Fossa dei Leoni*, or "The Lion's Den." The group broke up after some of its members were accused of stealing banners from another group. Today, Milan's main ultras groups are the *Brigate Rossonere*, or "The Red and Black Brigade," and the *Commandos Tigre*, or "Tiger Commandos." The Milan ultras groups have their own websites and social media pages. Some have YouTube channels where people can watch videos of their match-day activities.

Fan Traditions

#1 Scarves are a staple for AC Milan fans. They feature team colors, logos, and player names.

#2 Even though San Siro rules prohibit them, some Milan ultras groups use flares and colored smoke bombs to celebrate goals and saves during matches.

Legends of the Past

Many great players have suited up for Milan. A few of them have become icons of the team and the city it represents.

Position: Midfielder/Defender
Years in Pro Soccer: 1980–1995
Born: September 30, 1962, Amsterdam, Netherlands

Frank Rijkaard

Frank Rijkaard started playing professional soccer when he was only 18. Rijkaard started out with the Dutch team Ajax. He even scored a goal in his very first game. Rijkaard played for a few other professional teams before joining Milan. After joining the team, he scored 16 goals in 142 games. Rijkaard is considered one of the best defensive midfielders of his time. After he stopped playing, he went on to manage a number of professional and national teams.

Paolo Maldini

Paolo Maldini played with AC Milan for his entire professional career. Maldini is considered one of the greatest defenders of all time. He won 26 championship trophies with Milan. Maldini's nickname was *Il Capitano*, or "the Captain." He was part of coach Arrigo Sacchi's "Immortals" squad. Maldini led the team to eight trophies in four seasons. He also played in four World Cups with the Italian National Team. He is one of only 18 professional soccer players to make more than 1,000 career game appearances. Maldini retired in 2009. He is now co-owner of the North American Soccer League (NASL) club Miami FC.

Position: Defender
Years in Pro Soccer: 1985–2009
Born: June 26, 1968, Milan, Italy

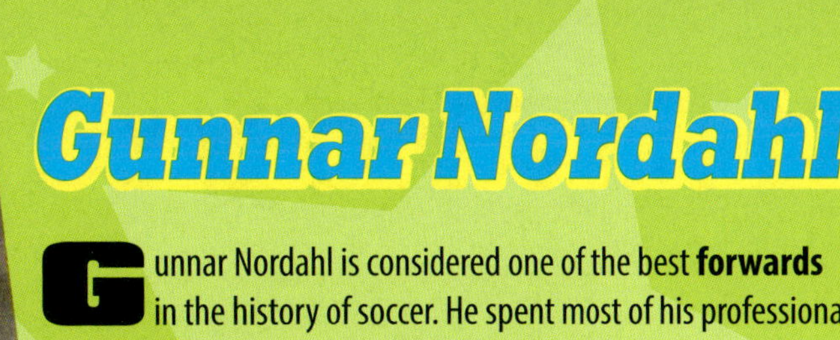

Gunnar Nordahl

Gunnar Nordahl is considered one of the best **forwards** in the history of soccer. He spent most of his professional career with Milan. Nordahl was part of the famous Gre-No-Li trio. This included fellow Swedes Gunnar Gren and Nils Liedholm. Nordahl's nickname was *Il Cannoniere*, or "the Gunner." He holds the record in Serie A as the top non-Italian goal scorer, with 210 goals. Nordahl was the highest goal scorer in Serie A in five different seasons. He also led Sweden to a gold medal in the 1948 Olympics.

Position: Forward
Years in Pro Soccer: 1937–1958
Born: October 19, 1921, Hörnefors, Sweden

Kaká

Kaká has been called one of the greatest soccer players of his generation. He played with Milan for seven seasons. Kaká made 287 game appearances and scored 101 goals for the team. He won the UEFA Champions League, the UEFA Super Cup, and the FIFA Club World Cup with Milan. Kaká was named Serie A Footballer of the Year in 2007. He was inducted into the AC Milan Hall of Fame in 2010.

Position: Midfielder
Years in Pro Soccer: 2001–2017
Born: April 22, 1982, Gama, Federal District, Brazil

Stars of Today

Milan's current team is made up of some of soccer's greatest players.

Position: Defender
Years in Pro Soccer: 2004–present
Born: September 30, 1986, Padilla, Colombia

Cristián Zapata

Cristián Zapata is a Colombian football player who signed with Milan in 2012. He is an intimidating defender because of his height, 6 feet, 1 inch (187 centimeters). Zapata is known for his skill at winning balls in the air. He averages 2.7 aerial balls won per game. Zapata is also skilled at controlling the ball and keeping it from the other team. He is naturally right-footed. However, his skill with both feet allows him to play many defensive positions. Zapata has been a member of the Colombian National Team since 2007. He played in the 2014 FIFA World Cup.

Giacomo Bonaventura

Giacomo Bonaventura is known as "Jack" to teammates and fans. He has played more than 200 games and scored more than 30 goals in the Serie A division. He transferred to Milan in 2014. Bonaventura said joining Milan was a dream come true. He is a gifted player who is comfortable in any midfield position. Bonaventura is well known for his ball skills. He creates many scoring opportunities for teammates. Due to his ability to strike from a distance, Bonaventura also scores frequently himself.

Position: Midfielder
Years in Pro Soccer: 2007–present
Born: August 22, 1989, San Severino Marche, Italy

Suso

Suso was born Jesús Joaquín Fernández Sáenz de la Torre. He played for Liverpool before joining Milan in 2014. Suso has scored more than 10 goals and has several assists for Milan. He also played for the Spanish National U-17, 18, 19, 20, and 21 teams. Suso is currently a member of the Spanish National team. He also played in a FIFA 2018 World Cup qualifying match against Italy. He is known for his quickness. Suso is good at multiple forward and midfield positions.

Position: Forward
Years in Pro Soccer: 2012–present
Born: November 19, 1993, Cádiz, Spain

Ignazio Abate

Ignazio Abate is known for his speed. Abate is considered one of the fastest football players in Europe. He joined Milan in 2004 but only played for one season. After playing for several other Italian clubs, he returned to Milan in 2009. Abate worked his way to a starting position after two seasons. He has now made more than 250 total game appearances for Milan. Abate is also a member of the Italian National Team. He played in the 2014 FIFA World Cup tournament against Costa Rica.

Position: Defender
Years in Pro Soccer: 2004–present
Born: November 12, 1986, Sant'Agata de Goti, Italy

All-Time Records

902

League Matches Played

Paolo Maldini played a record 902 league matches with AC Milan.

7

European Champions League Wins

AC Milan holds the record for European Champions League Cup wins by an Italian team.

221

Goals

During his time playing for Milan, Gunnar Nordahl scored 221 goals.

929

Minutes

Goalkeeper Sebastiano Rossi went 929 minutes, more than 11 matches, without giving up a single goal during the 1993–94 season.

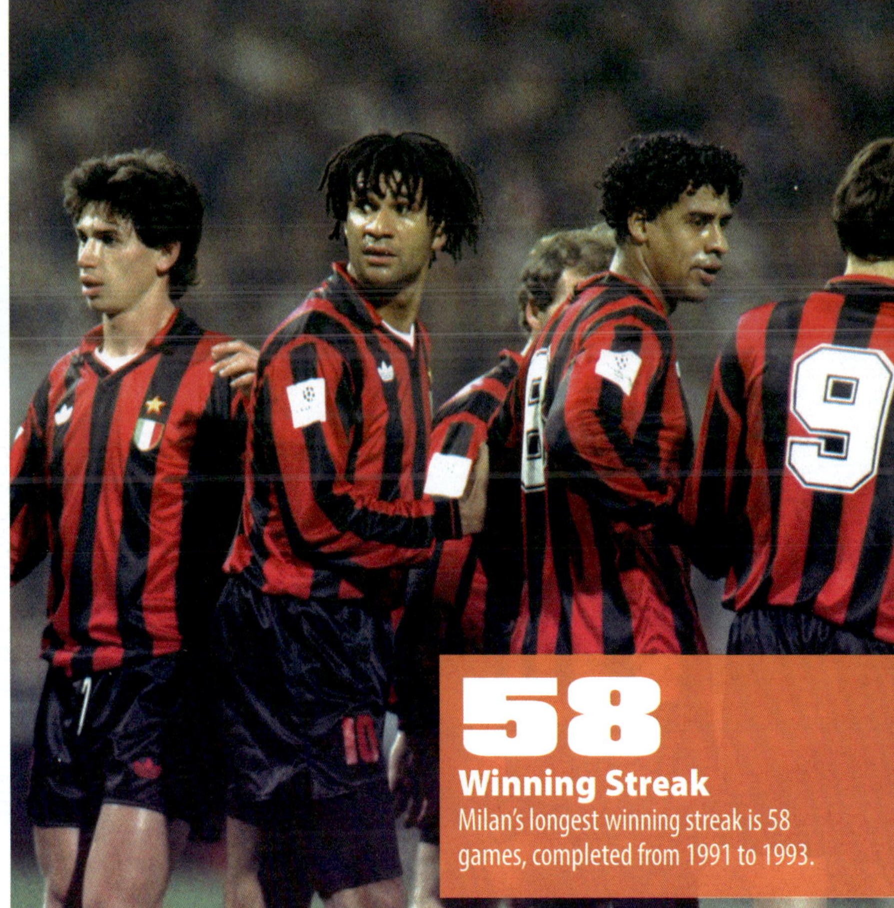

58

Winning Streak

Milan's longest winning streak is 58 games, completed from 1991 to 1993.

Timeline

Throughout the team's history, AC Milan has had many memorable events that have become defining moments for the team and its fans.

1899
The Milan Foot-Ball and Cricket Club is formed by Herbert Kiplin and Alfred Edwards.

1914
With the onset of World War I, play is halted for AC Milan and other European clubs until 1919.

1900 | 1910 | 1920 | 1930 | 1940 | 1950

1908
A disagreement leads to a split and the formation of Inter Milan, which remains AC Milan's fiercest rival.

In 1901, the club wins its first national title and a King's Medal.

1949
Gunnar Nordahl signs with Milan and leads the team in several successful seasons. Nordahl remains the team's record top scorer.

1967
Milan wins its first *Coppa Italia*, or "Italian Cup."

The Future
Milan has failed to qualify for championships in recent years. Former Italian prime minister Silvio Berlusconi was a longtime owner of the club. In 2017, he decided to sell it. Chinese investor Li Yonghong purchased Milan. He invested more than $700 million in the team. Yonghong vowed to make Milan the number-one club in the world and restore it to its former glory.

1960 1970 1980 1990 2000 2010

For the first time in club history, Milan wins a European title, the European Cup, in 1963.

1985
Paolo Maldini begins his first of 25 seasons with Milan.

1969
Coach Nereo Rocco's second coaching role with Milan leads the team to another European Cup and the team's first Intercontinental Cup.

Write a Biography

Life Story

A person's life story can be the subject of a book. This kind of book is called a biography. Biographies often describe the lives of people who have achieved great success. These people may be alive today, or they may have lived many years ago. Reading a biography can help you learn more about a great person.

Get the Facts

Use this book, and research in the library and on the internet, to find out more about your favorite player. Learn as much about him as you can. What position does he play? What are his statistics in important categories? Has he set any records? Also, be sure to write down key events in the person's life. What was his childhood like? What has he accomplished off the field? Is there anything else that makes this person special or unusual?

Use the Concept Web

A concept web is a useful research tool. Read the questions in the concept web on the following page. Answer the questions in your notebook. Your answers will help you write a biography.

Concept Web

Adulthood

- Where does this individual currently reside?
- Does he or she have a family?

Your Opinion

- What did you learn from the books you read in your research?
- Would you suggest these books to others?
- Was anything missing from these books?

Childhood

- Where and when was this person born?
- Describe his or her parents, siblings, and friends.
- Did this person grow up in unusual circumstances?

Accomplishments off the Field

- What is this person's life's work?
- Has he or she received awards or recognition for accomplishments?
- How have this person's accomplishments served others?

Write a Biography

Help and Obstacles

- Did this individual have a positive attitude?
- Did he or she receive help from others?
- Did this person have a mentor?
- Did this person face any hardships?
- If so, how were the hardships overcome?

Accomplishments on the Field

- What records does this person hold?
- What key games and plays have defined his career?
- What are his stats in categories important to his position?

Work and Preparation

- What was this person's education?
- What was his or her work experience?
- How does this person work?
- What is the process he or she uses?

Trivia Time

Take this quiz to test your knowledge of AC Milan. The answers are printed upside down under each question.

1 Who holds the record for the most game appearances with Milan?

A. Paolo Maldini

2 How many minutes did goalkeeper Sebastiano Rossi go without allowing a goal against Milan?

A. 929

3 What local team is Milan's biggest rival?

A. Inter Milan

4 What does the nickname *Rossoneri* mean?

A. The Red and Black

5 What color is Milan's away uniform?

A. White

6 How many matches did Nereo Rocco serve as a coach for Milan?

A. 459

7 What was Arrigo Sacchi's job before he became a football coach?

A. Shoe salesman

8 Who is Milan's all-time record goal scorer?

A. Gunnar Nordahl

9 What is the most number of matches Milan played without losing?

A. 58

Key Words

club: an athletic team or organization

derby: a game between two rivals or teams from the same town

FIFA: the *Fédération Internationale de Football Association*, or "International Federation of Association Football;" a private international organization that oversees professional soccer

football: what soccer is called in European countries

forward: a player on a soccer team who normally plays closest to the opponent's goal

goalkeepers: also called goalies. The players responsible for keeping the ball from going into the goal and the only players who are allowed to pick up the ball.

kit: the standard attire and equipment worn by soccer players, including a shirt, shorts, socks, and shin guards

memorabilia: objects that are collected because of historical importance to a person, group, or event

pitch: an area that is used for playing sports

scandal: a public event considered morally or legally wrong, leading to general outrage

Scudetto: the award given to the champions of Italy's top division of professional soccer

Serie A: the top professional soccer league in Italy

titles: championships

ultras: a type of football fan known for extreme support of a football club

Index

Log on to www.av2books.com

AV² by Weigl brings you media enhanced books that support active learning. Go to www.av2books.com, and enter the special code found on page 2 of this book. You will gain access to enriched and enhanced content that supplements and complements this book. Content includes video, audio, weblinks, quizzes, a slide show, and activities.

AV² Online Navigation

Audio
Listen to sections of the book read aloud.

Book Pages
AV² pages directly correspond to pages in the book.

Video
Watch informative video clips.

Embedded Weblinks
Gain additional information for research.

Key Words
Study vocabulary, and complete a matching word activity.

Try This!
Complete activities and hands-on experiments.

Quizzes
Test your knowledge.

Slide Show
View images and captions, and prepare a presentation.

AV² was built to bridge the gap between print and digital. We encourage you to tell us what you like and what you want to see in the future.

Sign up to be an AV² Ambassador at www.av2books.com/ambassador.

Due to the dynamic nature of the Internet, some of the URLs and activities provided as part of AV² by Weigl may have changed or ceased to exist. AV² by Weigl accepts no responsibility for any such changes. All media enhanced books are regularly monitored to update addresses and sites in a timely manner. Contact AV² by Weigl at 1-866-649-3445 or av2books@weigl.com with any questions, comments, or feedback.